T0351453

Sebastian Dreaming

THE GERMAN LIST

GEORG TRAKL

Sebastian Dreaming

Book Two of Our Trakl

TRANSLATED BY JAMES REIDEL

LONDON NEW YORK CALCUTTA

This publication was supported by a grant from
the Goethe-Institut India

Grateful acknowledgment is made to the following publications in
which the following translations originally appeared: *Mudlark* for
'To One Short-Lived'; *Verse* for 'Dream and Benightment', 'Trans-
figuration of Evil' and 'Winter Night'.

Seagull Books, 2016

ISBN 978 0 8574 2 331 3

British Cataloguing-in-Publication Data
A catalogue record for this book is available
from the British Library

Typeset in Adobe Caslon Pro by Seagull Books, Calcutta, India
Printed and bound at Maple Press, York, Pennsylvania, USA

Contents

The 'New Name'

On 17 May 1914, the Austrian writer Felix Braun contributed an article to the feuilleton of the Sunday Vienna *New Free Press*. In addition to profiles of Stefan George, Rainer Maria Rilke and Franz Werfel, Braun hailed Georg Trakl and his first book, simply titled *Poems* (1913). In Vienna's competitive literary world, Trakl had arrived. However, within less than six months, on 3 November, he was dead from an overdose of cocaine tablets or tincture in a military hospital where, only a few days earlier, he had learnt of a disappointment—the proofs of his second book *Sebastian Dreaming* would not be forthcoming due to the war.

A new name: Georg Trakl—and a new scene opens. The figure of the solitary dreamer, losing himself in a distant landscape, full of faces, staggering over a reeling earth, under a reeling sky, in a chaos of worlds collapsing into one another within and without; heighted states of drunkenness and visions, monstrous solitudes and barbarisms, primal voices of intensely natural events, pure resonations of the soul, melancholies of forgotten villages, nocturnal countrysides, the half-heard calls to life of man and beast which are full of the solitudes of tree and flower, the poet time and again, forsaken amid the world's thousandfold spell: [. . .] he does not project his will at anything, he wants nothing, as though wandering away, with his demons driving him, he is the drunkard facing the world, the ignes fatui luring one downward, the sweet beguiling voices, and the angels who appear to him, the corpses and souls.

Sebastian Dreaming

Childhood

Filled with elderberry fruit; childhood lived quietly
In a blue den. Over the vanished path,
Where the wild grass rustles brown now,
The still branches brood; the rustle of the leaves

A thing like when blue water is heard in the rocks.
The blackbird's lament is soft. A herdsman
Follows the sun speechless, which rolls off the autumn hill.

A blue blink of an eye is but a soul.
A timid deer shows itself at the forest's edge and peacefully
Old bells grow still in the valley and black hamlets.

More pious you know the meaning of these dark years,
A chill and autumn in lonely rooms;
And in a holier blue radiant steps peal forth.

An open window quietly rattles; the sight
Of the fallen cemetery on the hill brings tears,
A reminder of legends told; but sometimes the soul brightens
When it imagines a happy people, dark golden days of spring.

Hour Song

With dark looks the lovers regard themselves,
The blond ones, bright ones. In congealing darkness
Their yearning arms embrace emaciated.

The mouth of the one blest burst crimson. The wide eyes
Mirror the dark gold of the spring afternoon,
The forest's edge and blackness, fears of dusk in the green;
Perhaps an unspeakable flight of birds, the unborn's
Path towards gloomy villages, lonely summers
And from a fallen blue sometimes one who died appears.

The yellow grain rustles in the field.
This life is hard and the peasant's scythe swings of steel,
The carpenter joins massive beams.

The leaves turn crimson in the autumn, the monk-like spirit
Wanders through fine days; the grapes are ripe
And the air festive on vast farms.
The yellowed fruit smells sweet; subdued is the laughter
Of the gaiety, music and dance in beshadowed cellars;
In the darkening garden a step and stillness of the dead boy.

Underway

In the evening they carry the stranger into the deadhouse;
A smell of tar; the quiet rustle of red plane trees;
The dark flight of jackdaws; a guard detail paraded on the square.
In the adjoining room the sister plays a sonata by Schubert.
Her smile sinks quietly into the fallen fountain,
Which into the twilight purls blue. O, how old is our kind.
Someone whispers down in the garden; someone has departed
    this black sky.
The apples smell on the sideboard. Grandmother lights golden
    candles.

O, how warm is the autumn. Our footsteps quietly make sounds
    in the old park
Under the tall trees. O, how grim is the hyacinthine face of the
    twilight.
The blue spring at your feet, inscrutable the red stillness of your
    mouth,
Made sad by the sleep of the leaves, the dark gold of rotting
    sunflowers.
Your lids are heavy with poppies and quietly dream against my
    brow.
Softly bells shudder through the breast. A blue cloud
In the twilight your face has fallen on me.

A song for guitar, which resonates in a strange tavern,
The rank elderberry trees there, a long-gone November day,
Familiar steps on the darkening staircase, the sight of browned
    beams,
An open window in which a sweet hope lingered—
Which is all inexpressible, O God that one is brought to his
    knees broken.

O, how dark is this night. A crimson flame
Goes out in my mouth. In the stillness
The lonely strings of the uneasy soul die away.
Let go, when drunk on wine the head drops in the gutter.

Landscape

September evening; the dark calls of the shepherds echo
    mournfully
Through the darkening village; fire sprays inside the forge.
A black horse rears enormous; the hyacinthine curls of the
    country girl
Play for the ardour of his crimson nostrils.
The call of the doe quietly freezes at the edge of the forest
And the yellow flowers of autumn
Bend speechless over the blue face of the pond.
A tree bursts into red flames; the bats flutter upward with black
    faces.

To the Boy Elis

Elis, when the blackbird calls in the black forest,
This is your going down.
Your lips sip the cold of the blue mountain spring.

Let it be when your brow quietly bleeds
Archaic legends
And the dark augur of birds in the sky.

But you walk with such yielding steps into the night,
Which sags full of purple grapes
And you sway your arms handsome in the blue.

A thorn bush makes a sound
Where your moon eyes are.
O, how long, Elis, you have been dead.

Your body is a hyacinth,
In which a monk dips waxen fingers.
A black den is our silence,

From which a gentle beast appears at times
And slowly the heavy lids droop.
Upon your temples drips black dew,

The last gold of fallen stars.

Elis

1

Perfect is the stillness of this golden day.
Amid ancient oaks
You appear, Elis, one at rest with wide-open eyes.

Their blueness reflects the sleep of lovers.
On your mouth
Your pink sighs grow silent.

With evening the fisherman pulled in his black nets.
A good shepherd
Drives his flock to the forest's edge.
O! how righteous, Elis, are all your days.

Quietly falls
The blue stillness of the olive tree on bare walls,
An old man's dark song dies away.

A golden boat
Heaves your heart, Elis, in a lonely sky.

2

A soft glockenspiel beats in Elis' breast
In the evening,
Then his head sinks into the black pillow.

A blue deer
Quietly bleeds in the thorn brake.

A brown tree stands there detached;
Its blue fruit fell from it.

Signs and stars
Quietly sink into the pond of evening.

Over the hill it has become winter.

Blue doves
Drink the icy sweat at night
Beading down Elis' crystal brow.

Ever resounds
God's lonely wind on black walls.

Hohenburg

No one is home. Autumn in rooms;
Sonata of moonlight
And that awakening at the edge of the darkening forest.

Ever do you think the white face of man
Far from the fury of time;
Green branches bend willingly over one dreaming;

Cross and dusk;
Ascending towards unoccupied windows,
His star embraces the sound with crimson arms

Thus trembles the stranger in the dark,
Then he quietly lifts eyelids over some human thing
That is distant; the silver voice of the wind in the hallway.

Sebastian Dreaming

For Adolf Loos

1

Mother bore the babe in the white moon,
In the shadow of the walnuts, ancient elderberry,
Drunk on poppy juice, the lament of the thrush;
And silently
A bearded face bows with compassion over her

Quietly in the dark of the window; and the old chattel
Of ancestors
Lay broken up; love and autumn reverie.

So dark a day in the year, a sad childhood,
As the boy quietly descended into cool water, silver fish,
Calm and a face;
As he flung himself hard as stone in front of wild black horses,
His star came over him in a grey night;

Or when he, in the mother's freezing hand,
Walked about Saint Peter's autumn cemetery at dusk,
A frail corpse lay quiet in the dark of its cell
And it lifted cold lids above him.

But he was a little bird in the bare branches,
The long bells in the November evening,
The father's stillness, as he asleep descended winding stairs
    in twilight.

2

Peace for the soul. A lonely winter evening,
The dark shapes of the herdsmen at the old pond;
A baby in a cottage of straw; O how quiet
The face sank into a black fever.
Holy night.

Or when he, in the father's calloused hand,
Silently climbed the dark mountain of Calvary
And in the darkening niches of the rocks
The blue embodiment of man underwent his legend,
From the wound under the heart blood ran crimson.
O how quietly the cross stands erect in a dark soul.

Love; as the snow melted in black valleys,
A fair blue breeze picked itself up in the old elderberry,
In the shadowy canopy of the walnut tree;
And to the boy quietly appeared his pink angel.

Joy; as an evening sonata plays in cool rooms,
In the brown wood beams
A blue moth crawled from its silver cocoon.

O the closeness of death. Inside a stone wall
A yellow head bows, silencing the child,
As the moon decayed in that March.

3

Pink Easter daffodils in the mausoleum of night
And the silver voices of stars,
Such that a dark madness eased from the sleeper's brow in
      shivers.

O how still a path to the blue river
Contemplating forgotten things, while in the green branches
A thrush called a stranger in his going down.

Or when he, in the old man's bone hand,
Walked before the crumbling wall of the city at dusk
And that old man bore a pink babe in a black coat,
The spirit of evil appeared in the shadow of the walnut tree.

To feel across the green ascent of summer. O how quietly
The garden rotted in the brown stillness of the autumn,
That smell and melancholy of the old elderberry,
As the silver voice of the angel died in Sebastian's shadow.

On the Moor

Wanderer in the black wind; thin reeds whisper quietly
In the stillness of the moor. A flock of wild birds
Follows in the grey sky;
Crosswise over ominous waters.

Fury. In a fallen cottage
The decay flaps about with black wings;
Stunted birch trees sigh in the wind.

Evening in an empty tavern. The soft melancholy
Of grazing herds envelopes the way home,
Phenomenon of night: toads emerging from silver waters.

In the Spring

Quietly the snow gave with dark footsteps,
In the shade of the tree
The pink eyelids of lovers raise.

The dark calls of the boatmen are ever followed
By star and night;
And the oars beat quietly in rhythm.

Soon along a fallen wall bloom
The violets,
So still greens the temple of one alone.

Evening in Lans

Journey through a summer in twilight
Past sheaves of yellowed grain. Beneath whitewashed arches,
Where swallows flew in and out, we drank heady wine.

Beauty: O melancholy and crimson laughter.
Evening and the dark fragrances of the green
Cool our sweltering brows with chills.

Silver water runs over the steps of the forest,
The night and speechless a forgotten life.
Friend; the embowered footbridges to the village.

On the Mönchsberg

Where the fallen path descends into the shade of autumn elms,
Far from the cottages of leaves, sleeping shepherds,
All along the dark figure of the chill follows the wanderer

Across a bone footbridge, the hyacinthine voice of the boy,
Quietly telling the forgotten legend of the forest,
The wild lament of the brother, a sick thing more gentle now.

Thus a sparse green strikes the knee of the stranger,
The head turned stone;
The blue stream rushes closer the lamentations of the women.

Kaspar Hauser Song

For Bessie Loos

He really loved the sun, which descended the hill crimson,
The ways through the forest, the singing blackbird
And the joy of the green.

Sincere was his living in the shadows of trees
And straight his face.
God spoke a soft flame to his heart:
O man!

Silently his footsteps found the city by evening;
The dark wail of his mouth:
I want to be a horse soldier.

But bush and beast followed him,
A house and a twilight garden of white people
And his murderer asked to see him.

Spring and summer and beautiful the autumn
Of the just, his quiet step
By the dark rooms of dreamers.
At night he kept alone with his star;

Saw how snow fell into bare branches
And the shadow of the murderer in the darkening hall.

The unborn's head slumped silver.

By Night

The blue of my eyes is put out in this night,
The red gold of my heart. O! How still burns the candle.
Your blue mantle enfolds the one falling;
Your red mouth seals the friend's benightment.

Transfiguration of Evil

Autumn: long black steps at the forest's edge, a minute of mute devastation; the brow of the leper rises to hear under the leafless tree. An evening long gone that falls now over the ascent of moss; November. A bell tolls and the drover drives a herd of black and red horses into the village. Under the hazel tree the green hunter guts a deer. His hands steam with blood and the shadow of the beast in the leaves sighs at the eyes of the man, brown and guarded; the forest. Crows scattering; three. Their flight is like a sonata, full of faded chords and virile melancholy; quietly a golden cloud breaks up. Near the mill boys set a fire. Flame is the palest one's brother and the other laughs buried in his crimson hair; or it is a place of murder where a rocky road passes. The barberries are gone, it dreams the yearlong in the leaden air beneath the pines; fear, a green darkness, the gurgling of someone drowning: from the starry pond the fisherman hauls in a great black fish, face full of brutality and madness. The voices of the reeds, of men arguing in the back as that other rocks them in a red boat across cold autumn water, living in the dark tales of his kind and whose eyes stone hard gaped over the nights and maiden terrors. Evil.

What makes you to stand still on the falling stairs in your father's house? A leaden black. Why do you lift a silver hand to your eyes; and why do your lids sag as though drunk on poppies? Yet you see the starry sky through the wall of stone, the Milky Way, Saturn; red. The barren tree beats furiously on the wall of stone. You on falling steps: tree, star, stone! You, a blue animal quietly trembling; you, the pale priest who slaughters it on a black altar. O your smile in the dark, sad and evil, so that a child pales in its sleep. A red flame sprang from your hand and there a moth burned. O the flute of the candle; O the flute of death. What made you to stand still on the falling stairs in your father's house? At the gate below an angel taps with a crystal finger.

O the hell of sleep; a dark alley, brown gardens. Quietly the incarnation of the dead rings a bell in the blue evening. Green blossoms flit about her and her face has forsaken her. Or it bows faded over the cold brow of the murderer in the dark of the hallway; worship; crimson flame of lust; the sleeper falls dying across black steps into the dark.

Somebody left you at the crossroads and you take a long look back. Silver footsteps in the shade of a stunted apple tree. The fruit brightens crimson in the black branches and in the grass the snake sheds its skin. O! The dark, the sweat coming to your icy brow and the sad dreams in the wine, in that village tavern under black smoke-filled beams. You, still a wilderness, who conjures the pink islands from the brown tobacco smoke and draws from inside the wild scream of a griffin as it hunts black cliffs at sea, in storm and ice. You, some green metal and a fiery face inside which wants to go off and sing of dark times from a pile of bones and the flaming fall of the angels. O! Despair bending a knee with a silent cry.

A dead man calls on you. From the heart flows the self-drawn blood and an inexpressible moment nests in a black eyebrow; dark meeting. You—a crimson moon while the other one emerges in the green shadow of the olive tree. Whom the imperishable night follows.

The Autumn of One Alone

In the Park

Once more strolling in the old park,
O! Silent yellow and red flowers.
You grieve too, you gentle deities,
And the autumn gold of the elms.
At the blue pond loom motionless
The reeds, the thrush quiets with dusk.
O! Lower your forehead too then
For the ancestors' fallen marble.

A Winter Evening

When snow falls at the window,
The evening bells toll a long time,
The table's prepared for many
And the house well appointed.

A few in their wandering
On dark paths arrive at the gate.
Golden grows the tree of mercy
From the cold sap of the earth.

A wayfarer enters silent;
Pain changed the threshold into stone.
Then there glows in a purer light
Bread and wine on the table.

The Damned

1

It grows dark. The old women go to the well.
A red laughs in the darkness of the chestnuts.
The aroma of bread pours from a shop
And sunflowers lower over the fence.

The inn by the river still sounds soft and low.
Guitars serenade; a chink of money.
A holy light falls upon that little girl,
Waiting outside the glass door meek and white.

O! The blue glow she quickens in the panes,
Framed by the thorns, black and fixed in rapture.
A hunched-over scribbler smiles as though mad
Into the water quenching a wild rage.

2

With evening the plague fringes her blue cloak
And an ominous guest throws the gate's bolt.
The maple's black burden falls through the window;
A boy lays his forehead into her hand.

Her lids often lower cruel and heavy.
The child's hands are running through her hair
And his tears are streaming down hot and clear
Into the holes of her eyes black and void.

A nest of scarlet-coloured serpents rears
Lethargically in her churning womb.
The arms let go of what is dying away,
Which the carpet's melancholy fringes.

3

In the brown garden a glockenspiel plays.
A blue hangs in the dark of the chestnuts,
The sweet-smelling cloak of a strange woman.
Scent of mignonettes; and feeling a glow

Of evil. The drenched brow bows cold and pale
Over the refuse, in which the rat digs,
Bathed by the warm scarlet blaze of the stars;
In the garden apples thud dull and soft.

The night is black. Like a wraith the foehn blows
The white nightshirt of the wandering boy
And in his mouth quietly grabs the hand
Of the dead. Sonia smiles softly and sweet.

Sonia

Dusk returns in an old garden;
Sonia's life, a blue silence.
Wild birds in wandering passage;
A bare tree in fall and silence.

A sunflower softly lowers,
Bending over Sonia's white life.
A wound, red, never revealed
In dark rooms allows for a life.

Wherever blue bells are tolling;
Sonia's footsteps and soft silence.
A dying beast greets slipping by,
A bare tree in fall and silence.

A sun of days long ago shines
Down upon Sonia's white brows,
Snow, that is making her cheeks wet,
And the wild country of her brows.

Along

Grain and grapes have been cut,
The hamlet in autumn and peace.
Hammer and anvil clang ceaselessly,
Laughter in crimson foliage.

Fetch the white child
Asters from the dark fences.
Speak of how long we have died;
Sunlight wants to come blackly out.

A small red fish in the pond;
A brow, which listens in fear;
Evening wind hums low at the window,
A blue barrel organ.

A star and a furtive glimmer
Make for peering up once more.
The mother's apparition in pain and dread;
Black mignonettes in the dark.

Autumn Soul

Hunter's horn, baying for blood;
Behind a cross and a brown hill
The pond's surface gradually blinds,
The hawk screeches sharp and shrill.

Across stubble field and path
A black silence is now afraid;
A clear sky inside the branches;
Just the brook runs soft and still.

Soon fish and deer slip away.
A blue soul, a dark wandering
Soon split us from dear ones, others.
Evening shifts sense and likeness.

A righteous life's bread and wine,
Into your merciful hands
God places the dark end of man,
All guilt and red agony.

Afra

A child with brown hair. A prayer and amen
Silently darken over the evening chill
And Afra's smile red in a yellow frame
Of sunflowers, fear and grey oppressiveness.

Wrapped inside a blue mantle the monk saw her
From times past piously painted on stained glass;
Who still bids to be kindly led off in pain—
When her stars go haunting through his blood.

Autumn sunset; the elderberries' silence.
The blue motion of the water lifts the brow,
Laid out over a bier a shroud made of hair.

The rotting fruit is falling from the branches;
The birds in flight are untold, a gathering
With the dying; who the dark years follow.

The Autumn of One Alone

The dark autumn comes in ripe fruit and plenty,
A yellowed glow from beautiful summer days.
A pure blue emerges from a rotting husk;
The birds on the wing resound of ancient lore.
The wine grapes have been pressed, the mellow silence
Fills with the quiet answers to dark questions.

And here and there a cross on a bleak hilltop;
A flock disappears into the red forest.
The cloud drifts over the surface of a pond;
The peasant's calm manner of gesture ceases.
The evening's blue wing stirs very quietly
A rooftop thatched with withered straw, the black earth.

Soon the stars nest in the brows of the weary;
In chilly parlours a silent humbling comes
And angels quietly emerge from the blue
Eyes of the lovers who more softly suffer.
The reeds are rustling; a bone horror assails
When the dew drips black from the leafless willows.

Song Septet of Death

Peace and Silence

Shepherds buried the sun in the leafless forest.
A fisherman pulled
The moon from the freezing pond in a net of hair.

In blue crystal
Lives the pale man whose cheek rests against his stars;
Or he nods his head in crimson sleep.

Yet the black flight of the birds always stirs
The beholder, the saint of blue flowers,
The stillness near recalls forgotten things, extinguished angels.

Once more the brow nights over in lunar stone;
A shining boy
The sister appears in autumn and black corruption.

Anif

Memory: gulls, gliding across the dark sky
Of a manly despair.
You live silently in the shadow of the autumn ashes,
Lost in the hill's fair measure;

Always you go down to the green river
When evening comes,
Echoing love; the dark deer peacefully encounters

A pink man. Drunk on the blue weather
The forehead stirs the dying leaves
And recalls the earnest face of the mother;
O, how everything sinks into the dark;

The stark rooms and the old chattel
Of ancestors.
This convulses the breast of the stranger.
O, you signs and stars.

Great is the guilt of the born. Woe, you golden throes
Of death,
As the soul dreams colder flowers.

The night bird ever calls in the bare branches
Above the moon's footstep,
An icy wind is heard at the village walls.

Birth

Mountains: black, silence and snow.
Red from the forest the chase descends;
O, the moss-hoared stares of the deer.

Silence of the mother; under black firs
The sleeping hands open up
As the cold moon comes out fallen.

O, the birth of men. At night rushes
Blue water in a rock gorge;
Sighing the fallen angel beholds his image.

Something pale wakes in a stifling parlour.
Two moons
Shine in the eyes of an old stone-hard woman.

Woe, the labouring mother's scream. With a black wing
The night touches the boy on the temple,
Snow, that falls quietly from purple clouds.

Going Down

To Karl Borromaeus Heinrich

Over the white pond
The wild birds are pulling away.
With evening an icy wind blows from our stars.

Over our graves
The shattered brow of the night bows.
Under the oaks we rock in a silver boat.

The white walls of the city always sound.
Under arching thorns
O my brother we climb blind hands of a clock to midnight.

To One Short-Lived

O, the black angel, who quietly emerged from the heart of the
    tree
When we were gentle playmates during the evening,
At the edge of the blue fountain.
Our step was steady, wide eyes in the brown chill of autumn,
O, the purple sweetness of the stars.

But this other there went down the stone steps of the
    Mönchsberg,
A blue smile in his face and strangely spun to a cocoon
In his more quiet childhood, and died;
And the silver face of this friend lingered in the garden,
Listening in the leaves or from inside ancient stones.

A soul sang the death, the green corruption of the flesh
And it was the rushing of the woods,
The keen plaintive cries of wild deer.
The blue bells of evening ever clang from darkening towers.

An hour came, when this other saw the shadows in the crimson
    sun,
The shadows of the decay in bare branches;

Evening, when the blackbird sang on a darkening wall.
The ghost of one short-lived silently appears in the room.

O, the blood that trickles from the throat of that intoning,
A blue flower; O, the fiery teardrop
Wept in the night.

Golden cloud and time. In a lonely cell
You more often bid the dead for one's guest,
Walk in intimate dialogue under elms down the green river.

Ghostly Twilight

Stillness meets at the edge of the woods
A dark deer;
On the hill the evening wind quietly ends,

The blackbird's lament trails off,
And the soft pipes of autumn
Fall silent in the reeds.

On a black cloud
Drunk from poppies you sail
The night pond,

The starry sky.
The sister's lunar voice forever echoes
Through the ghostly night.

Evening Land Song

O, the soul of a nocturnal wing beat:
Shepherds we once walked alongside darkening forests
And the red deer followed, the green flowers, and the purling
    stream
Full of humility. O, that primal sound of crickets,
Blood flowering on the sacrificial stone
And the cry of the lonely bird above the green stillness of the
    pond.

O, you crusades and fiery torments
Of the flesh, falling of crimson fruit
In the evening garden, where the pious youth of times past
    walked,
Fighting men now, waking from wounds and starry dreams.
O, the soft cyan sheaf of night.

O, you times of silence and golden autumns,
When we peaceful monks pressed the purple grapes;
And all around hill and forest shone.
O, you hunting parties and palaces; peace of evening,
Where man in his cell contemplated the righteous,
Grappled in silent prayer for God's living head.

O, the bitter hour of sundown,
As we contemplate a stone face in black waters.
But the lovers lift radiant silver eyelids:
One kind. Incense streams from pink pillows
And the sweet singing of the risen.

Apotheosis

When evening comes,
A blue face quietly leaves you.
A little bird sings in the tamarind tree.

A gentle monk
Folds dead hands.
A white angel visits Mary.

A night garland
Of violets, grain and purple grapes
Is the year of the beholder.

At your feet
The graves of the dead open
When you place your brow in silver hands.

Silently dwells
The autumn moon on your mouth,
Dark chanting drunk on poppy sap;

A blue flower,
That is softly heard in yellowed rock.

Foehn

Blind lament in the wind, moon winter days,
Childhood, quietly the footfalls fade away at a black hedge,
Long evening bells.
Quietly the white night comes drawn out,

Changing pain and worry of a stone-hard life
Into a crimson dream,
Such that the thorn needle is never pulled from the rotting body.

Deep in sleep the anxious soul breathes a sigh,

Deep the wind in the broken trees,
And there stumbles the plaintive figure
Of the mother through the lonely forest

Of this silent grief; Nights,
Full of tears, fiery angels.
A child's skeleton is dashed silver against a bare wall.

The Wanderer

The white night ever leans upon the hill,
Where the poplars loom in silver tones,
Are stars and stones.

Sleeping the footbridge arches over the torrent,
A dead face follows the boy,
Sickle moon in a pink gorge

Far from lauding shepherds. In ancient stones
The toad watches from its crystal eye,
The florid wind awakes, the birdsong of the deathlike
And the footsteps green quietly in the forest.

This is reminiscent of tree and beast. A slow ascent of moss;
And the moon,
That sinks radiant into sad waters.

The other returns once more and wanders to green shores,
Rocking aboard a black gondola through the fallen city.

Karl Kraus

White high priest of truth,
Crystal voice in which lives God's ice breath,
Angry magi,
Under his flaming coat chinks the blue mail of the warrior.

To the Fallen Silent

O, the madness of the great city, when with evening
Stunted trees bristle along a black wall,
The spirit of evil peers from a silver mask;
Light with a magnetic scourge drives out the stone night.
O, the lost peal of the evening bells.

Whore, who bore a dead baby with icy shivers.
In fury God's anger scourges the brow of the possessed,
Crimson plague, hunger, which bursts green eyes.
O, the horrific laughter of gold.

But mankind silently bleeds in a dark cave more speechless,
The redeeming head is welded from hard metals.

Passion

When Orpheus strums the lyre silver,
Lamenting one dead in the evening garden,
Who are you, one reposed, under towering trees?
The autumn reeds rustle with the lament,
The blue pond,
Dying away under greening trees
And following the shadow of the sister;
Dark love
Of a wild kind,
For whom the day rushes by on golden spokes.
Silent night.

Under dark firs
Two wolves mixed their blood
In a stone embrace; a goldness,
The cloud trailed away over the footbridge,
Patience and silence of childhood.
Once more the tender corpse meets
At the pool of Triton
Sleeping in his hyacinthine hair.
That that cold head would at last burst apart!

For a blue deer ever follows,
A thing peering under the trees in twilight,
These dark paths
Waking and moved by sweet night melodies,
Semi-madness;
Or there sounds a dark rapture
Filled with strings
Played at the cold feet of her the penitent
In the stone city.

Song Septet of Death

The spring dims blue; beneath trees running sap
Something dark wanders during dusk and sunset,
Listening to the soft plaintive cry of the blackbird.
The night comes on silent, a bleeding deer,
That slowly drops on the hill.

In the wet wind an apple branch in blossom sways,
Entangled things free themselves,
Dying away from night eyes; falling stars;
A gentle childhood song.

Coming more in view the sleeper came down from the
    black forest,
And a blue spring rushes in its bed,
So that the other there quietly raises the pale eyelids
Of his snowy face;

And the moon hunted a red beast
From his den;
And the dark lament of the women died in sighs.

More shining the white stranger lifted hands
Towards his star;
In silence a corpse leaves the fallen house.

O mankind's rotted shape: welded from cold metal,
Night and a terror of drowned forests
And the searing wilderness of the beast;
Dead calm of the soul.

The other one there sails down a shimmering river in a
    black boat,
Full of crimson stars, and the branches in leaf
Drop peacefully upon him,
Poppies from silver clouds.

Winter Night

Snow fell. After midnight you depart drunk on the crimson wine in the dark precinct of men, that red flame of their hearth. O the gloom!

Black frost. The earth is hard, the air tastes bitter. Your stars form ominous signs.

With steps turned to stone you stamp on the railroad ballast with wide eyes like a soldier who storms a black trench. *Avanti!*

Bitter snow and moon!

A red wolf which an angel strangles. Your bones clatter striding like blue ice and a smile full of grief and arrogance as turned your face to stone and the brow pales before the lust of the cold;

or bows silently over the sleep of a gatekeeper who sank into his wooden box.

Cold and smoke. A white starry shirt sears the supporting shoulders and God's vultures tear apart your metal heart.

O the stone hill. The cold body melts still and forgotten into the silver snow.

Black is sleep. The ear long follows the paths of stars in the ice.

Upon awakening the bells clang in the village. From the east gate the pink day entered silver.

Song of the Solitary

In Venice

Stillness in the night room.
The candlestick flickers silver
Before the chanting breath
Of the alone;
Incantatory clouds of rose.

A blackish swarm of flies
Clouds the stone space
And transfixed by the pain
Of the golden day is the head
Of the homeless.

Motionless the sea nights over.
A star and a black crossing
Vanished on the canal.
Child, your sickly smile
Follows me quietly to sleep.

Limbo

Along autumnal walls, there shadows search
The ringing gold on the hill,
Evening clouds herding
In the peace of withered plane trees.
This time breathes darker tears,
Damnation, as the dreamer's heart
Overflows from the crimson evening glow,
The gloom of the smoking city;
A golden chill drifts from the graveyard
After the strider, the stranger,
As though a fragile corpse followed in his shadow.

Quietly this stone structure tolls;
The garden of the orphans, the dark hospital,
A red ship on the canal.
Dreaming in the darkness stand and fall
Rotting people
And from black gates
Angels emerge with cold brows;
Blueness, mothers keening for the dead.
Through their long hair turns
A fiery wheel, the full day
Of the earth's pain without end.

In frigid rooms with no purpose
Chattels moulder, with bone hands
An unholy childhood
Gropes in the blue for fairy tales,
The fat rat gnaws door and coffer,
A heart
Freezes in snowy silence.
The crimson curses of hunger
Reverberate through the foul darkness,
The black swords of the lie,
Like a bronze gate being battered.

The Sun

The yellow sun comes over the hill daily.
The forest is beautiful, the dark beast,
Man; hunter or herdsman.

The fish breaches red in the green pond.
Under the domed sky
The fisherman quietly sails in the blue boat.

Slowly the grapes ripen, the grain.
When the day dwindles silently,
Something good and evil is caused.

When it becomes night,
The wanderer quietly lifts heavy eyelids;
Sun bursts from a dark gorge.

Song of a Caged Blackbird

For Ludwig von Ficker

Dark breath in green branches.
Small blue flowers sail about the face
Of the one alone, the golden step
Dying under the olive tree.
The night flutters upward with drunken wings.
Humility bleeds so quietly,
Dew that drips slowly from the budding thorn.
Shining arms of mercy
Embrace a breaking heart.

Summer

With evening ends the lament
Of the cuckoo in the woods.
The grain leans lower,
The red poppies.

A black storm threatens
Over the hill.
The old song of the crickets
Dies away in the field.

The leaves of the chestnut
Never stir.
On the winding stair
Your dress swishes.

The candle shines silent
In the dark room;
A silver hand
Snuffed it out;

A wind-still, starless night.

Remnants of Summer

So quiet has the green summer
Become, your crystal face.
Flowers die by the evening pond,
A terrified blackbird's call.

Vain hope of life. Already in the house
The swallow prepares for a journey
And the sun descends on the hill;
Already the night signals a starry passage.

Stillness of the village; Lonely woods
Are heard all around. Heart,
Lower yourself tenderly now,
Over her the peaceful sleeper.

So quiet has the green summer
Become and the footstep tolls
Of the stranger through the silver night.
A blue deer would remember his path,

The harmony of his ghostly year!

Year

Dark stillness of childhood. Amid greening ash trees
Feeds the gentleness of a blue gaze; golden peace.
The smell of violets delights a thing dark; tossing ears of grain
In the dusk, seeds and the golden shadow of melancholy.
The carpenter hews wood beams; in the darkening background
The mill grinds; in the hazel leaves a crimson mouth contorts,
A manly presence bent red over the silent water.
The autumn is quiet, the spirit of the forest; a golden cloud
Follows the alone, the black shadow of the grandchild.
Dwindling in a stone room; amid ancient cypresses
The tears' scenes for the night are gathered at the spring;
Golden eye of the beginning, dark patience of the end.

Evening Land
Else Lasker-Schüler in adoration

1

A moon, as if a thing dead
Emerged from a blue den,
And a great many blossoms
Fall across the rock path.
A thing sick weeps silver
By the evening's pond,
In a black boat
Lovers died across.

Or the footsteps toll
Of Elis through the grove,
The hyacinthine,
Once more to fade among oaks.
O the boy's figure
Formed from crystal tears,
Shadows in the night.
Jagged lightning illuminates a temple,
The one forever cold,
When on the greening hill
A spring storm sounds.

2

So quiet are the green forests
Of our home,
The crystal wave
Dying away at the fallen wall
And we wept in our sleep;
Wandering with halting steps
Along the thorn hedge
Singing in the summer of the evening,
In holy peace
Of the far shining vineyard;
Shadows now in the cold womb
Of the night, a grieving eagle.
So quietly a lunar radiance heals
The crimson wounds of melancholy.

3

You great cities
Built of stone
In the plain!
So speechless follows
The homeless
With a dark brow to the wind,
Leafless trees on the hill.
You broad rivers in twilight!
An eerie red sunset
In the storm clouds
Casts vast fear.
You dying people!
A pale wave
Crashing on shore of night,
Falling stars.

Spring of the Soul

Crying out in sleep; the wind dashes through the black streets,
The blue of spring beckons with breaking branches,
The purple night's dew and the surrounding stars go out.
The river dawns green, the old boulevards silver
And the towers of the city. O mild drunkenness
In the gliding boat and the dark calls of the blackbird
In childhood gardens. Already the pink veil is lifting.

The waters rush stately. O the wet shadows of the flood meadow,
The pacing animal; things greening, branches in blossom
Stirred by the crystal brow; a rocking boat shimmering.
The sun silently echoes in the pink clouds on the hill.
Vast is the stillness of the fir forest, stern shadows by the river.

Immaculate! Immaculate! Where are the appalling paths of the
    dead,
Of that grey stone silence, the rocks of night
And shadows without peace? A radiant solar abyss.

Sister, when I found you in a lonely clearing
In the forest and it was noon and the great silence of the beasts;
White among wild oaks, and the thorn buds silver.

A vast dying and the singing flame in the heart.
The waters flow darker about the beautiful play of the fish.

An hour of sorrow, a silent spectacle of the sun;
The soul is a strange thing on the earth. Ghostly a blueness
Dawns over the timbered forest and a dark bell
Rings long in the village; a peaceful cortege.
The myrtle blossoms in silence over the white eyelids of the
    dead.

Quietly the waters sound in the dwindling afternoon
And the wilderness greens darker on the bank, joy in a pink
    wind;
The soft singing of the brother on the evening hill.

In the Darkness

The soul keeps the blue spring season silent.
Under the wet branches of evening
The forehead dropped on each lover in shivers.

O the greening cross. In dark speech
Man and woman recognized each other.
Along a bare wall
The alone wanders in his stars.

Over the moon-dappled trails in the forest
The wilderness sank
Of forgotten game; a glimpse of blue
Breaks from falling cliffs.

Song of the Solitary
To Karl Borromaeus Heinrich

Filled with harmonies is the flight of birds. With evening
The green forests gather at cottages more still;
The crystal pastures of deer.
Something dark soothes the purling of the brook, the wet
shadows

And the flowers of the summer, which sound beautiful in
the wind.
Already the brow dawns on the contemplative man.

And a small lamp lights, the good, in his heart
And the peace of the meal; for bread and wine are blessed
By God's hands, and the brother silently watches you
From nighted eyes, so he can rest from his thorny wanderings.
O that dwelling in the inspirited blue of the night.

Tenderly too, the silence in the room enfolds the ancestral
shadows,
The crimson tortures, the lament of a great line,
Which meekly dies out in the lone descendent.

For at the stone-hard threshold the forbearing wakes
ever radiant
From black minutes of insanity

And the cold blue enfolds him sweepingly and the bright
    dwindling of autumn,

The still house and the lore of the forest,
Measure and law and the lunar paths of the solitary.

Dream and Benightment

Dream and Benightment

With evening the father turned into an old man; in dark rooms the face of the mother became stone and the curse of a degenerate family lay on the boy. Sometimes he recalled his childhood full of sickness, terrors and darkness, of secret games in the starry garden, or that he fed rats in the twilit courtyard. From a blue mirror stepped the slender figure of the sister and he plunged into the dark as though dead. During the night his mouth split like rotten fruit and the stars glittered over his inexpressible sorrow. His dreams filled the ancient house of his fathers. With evening he was fond of walking through the fallen cemetery, or viewing the corpses in the twilit deadhouse, the green dapple of decay on their beautiful hands. At the gate of the cloister, he begged for a piece of bread; the shadow of a black horse sprang from the darkness and terrified him. As he lay in the cold bed, untold tears overwhelmed him. But there was no one who would have placed a hand on his brow. When autumn came, he walked, a clairvoyant, in brown bottomland. O, the hours of wild ecstasy, the evenings along a green river, the quests. O, the soul that quietly sang the song of the yellowed reeds; fiery piousness. He looked silently and long into the starry eyes of the toads, felt with trembling hands the coolness of the old stone and conjured the sacred lore of the blue spring. O the silver fish and the fruit that fell from stunted trees. The chords of his strides filled him with pride and misanthropy. On the way home he encountered an uninhabited palace. Fallen gods stood in the garden, mourning away in the evening. But to him it seemed: I lived forgotten years here. An organ chorale filled him with the awe of God. But in a dark den he misspent his days, lied and stole and concealed himself, a flaming wolf before the white face of his mother. O, the hour when he descended into the starry garden with a stone mouth, the shadow of the murderer came over him. With a crimson brow he walked in the moor and God's wrath caned his metal shoulders; O, the birches in the storm, the dark beasts that avoided his benighted paths. Hate scorched his heart, lust. Then he stepped into the green of the summer garden in the guise of a silent child, in whom he recognized his benighted face shining. Woe, the evening at the window, when a grey skeleton emerged from crimson flowers, death. O, you towers and bells; and the shadows of the night fell upon him as stone.

No one loved him. A lie scorched his head and unnatural acts in twilit rooms. The blue bustle of a woman's skirts made him stiffen into a pillar and in the door stood the figure of his mother by night. The shadow of evil rose above his head. O, you nights and stars. With evening he went away with the cripple on the mountain; the pink glow of the red evening sky lay on an icy peak and his heart sounded quietly in the twilight. The stormy firs sagged heavily above them and the red hunter emerged from the forest. As night fell, his heart shattered like crystal and the darkness pounded at his brow. Under the leafless oak trees, he strangled a feral cat with his icy hands. To his right the white figure of an angel appeared to protest and the shadow of the cripple waxed in the dark. But he picked up a stone and threw it at the other so that he fled howling, and the gentle face of the angel vanished sighing in the shadows of the trees. He lay long in the stony field and watched astonished at the golden tent of the stars. Chased by bats, he ran off into the dark. Breathless he entered the fallen house. In the courtyard he drank, a wild animal, from the blue waters of the well, until it froze him. Feverish he sat upon icy steps raging at God how he would die. O, the grey face of terror as he looked up with wide eyes over a dove's slit throat. Darting up strange stairs he met a Jewish girl and grabbed her black hair and he took her mouth. A thing hostile followed him through the dark streets and an icy rattle gashed his ear. Along autumn walls, an altar boy, he followed the silent priest in silence; under withered trees he breathed the scarlet of the other's sacred robes intoxi-cated. O, the fallen disc of the sun. Sweet tortures partook of his flesh. In a desolate passage, his bloody figure appeared to him matted with dirt. He cherished deeply the august work of the stone; the tower, which with hellish faces stormed the blue starry sky at night; the cool grave in which mankind's fiery heart is upheld. Woe, the untold guilt which this signifies. But when he went down to the autumn river among the leafless trees contemplating this glowing thing, there appeared to him a flaming demon in a cloak of hair, the sister. On waking the stars went out above their heads.

O, cursed breed. When every fate is consummated in filthy rooms, death enters the house with mouldering footsteps. O, that spring was outside and a lovely bird might sing in the blossoming tree. But the sparse green withers grey at the window of those who come by night and the bleeding hearts still think about evil. O, the darkening spring paths of the contemplative. The hedge in flower pleases him as more just, the young seed of the peasant and the singing bird, God's gentle creature; the evening bells and the beautiful community of humankind. Thus he pardoned his fate and the stinging thorns. Unobstructed the brook greened where his foot wandered silver, and a telling tree rustled above his benighted head. Thus he raised with a slender hand the serpent, and with fiery tears his heart thawed. The silence of the forest is exalted, the greening darkness and the mossy beasts fluttering upwards when night falls. O, the chill, when each thing knows its guilt, takes a thorny path. Thus he found the white shape of the child in the thorn bush, bloody from the cloak of its bridegroom. But he stood mute, buried in his steely hair, and suffering for her. O, the shining angels, who scattered the night wind. He spent the night in a crystal cave and the leprosy waxed silver on his brow. A shadow walked the bridle path under autumn stars. Snow fell, and a blue darkness filled the house. Someone blind called with the hard voice of the father and summoned the horror. Woe the stooped appearance of the women. Under stiffened hands the fruit and chattel of the horrified descendants rotted. A wolf tore apart the firstborn and the sisters fled into dark garden to gaunt old men. The other one, a benighted voyant, sang by fallen walls and God's wind swallowed his voice. O, the lust of death. O, you children of a dark race. The evil flowers of blood shimmer silver on every temple, the cold moon in his shattered eyes. O, who come by night, O, the cursed.

In dark poisons the sleep is deep, filled by stars and the white face of the mother, which turned to stone. Death is bitter, the diet of the guilt-laden; the clay faces crumbled grinning in the brown branches of their tree. But the other one sang quietly in the green shadows of the elderberry, after he woke from bad dreams; this sweet playmate, a pink angel, approached him, so that he, a gentle deer, slept through the night; and he saw the starry face of purity. The sunflowers sagged golden over the garden fence as it turned summer. O, the industry of bees and the green leaves of the walnuts; the passing storm. The poppies grew silver as well, our starry night dreams born in their green bulbs. O, how still was the house, as the father went away into darkness. The fruit ripened crimson on the tree and the gardener lifted hard hands; O, the signs made of hair in the shining sun. With evening, however, the shadow of the dead silently entered the mourning circle of his family and its step rang of crystal across the green meadow before the forest. The silent gathered themselves at the table; with hands washed the dying brought them bread, bleeding. In the sister's stone eyes the hurt as her madness appeared on the ever night brow of the brother at supper, as the mother turned bread into stone under suffering hands. O, the rotting when they, with silver tongues, silence hell. Thus the lamps are put out in the cold chamber and from crimson masks the grieving look on in silence. A rain hissed the nightlong and refreshed the entrance hall. In a wilderness of thorns the darkness followed the yellowed path through the grain, the song of the lark and the gentle stillness of the green branches, so that he would find peace. O, you villages and mossy ascents, a shining view. But the bone steps stumble over the sleeping serpent at the forest's edge and the ear always follows the furious cry of the vulture. With evening he found a stony wasteland, a cortege for one dead into the house of the father. Crimson clouds enshrouded his head, so that he assaulted his own blood and image, a lunar face; then in a shattered mirror, sinking into emptiness like stone, a dying youth, the sister appeared, the cursed sex the night swallowed.

Notes

Page 1 | 'The "New Name"'

From Felix Braun, 'Georg Trakl' in 'Lyrische Gestalten und Begabungen' (Lyric Figures and Talents), *Neue Freie Presse* (Vienna *New Free Press*) (17 May 1914): 33.

Page 6 | 'Hour Song'

Title, *Hour Song*, from the German *Stundenlied*, a rhymed prayer or litany that follows the pious example of the Divine Office, such as the hourly hymns or calls of nightwatchmen.

Line 4, *one blest* (*Gesegneten*), this can be idiom, too, for a woman 'blest' with child, one who has received last rites and so on.

Page 7 | 'Underway'

Line 1, *deadhouse*, a cemetery morgue, often refrigerated with ice, where corpses are stored and displayed prior to burial.

Page 9 | 'Landscape'

Second version

Page 10 | 'To the Boy Elis'

Title, *Elis*, one of Trakl's personae derived from the 1819 short story 'Die Bergwerke von Falun' (The Mines of Falun) by E. T. A. Hoffmann, in which the hero is renamed Elis Fröbom, and Hugo von Hofmannsthal's 1899 dramatic adaptation, *Das Bergwerk zu Falun* (The Mine at Falun), which are based on the legend of the seventeenth-century Swedish miner Fets-Mats, who fell to his death down a mineshaft and whose perfectly preserved body was identified years later by his aged fiancée.

Page 11 | 'Elis'

Third version

Line 3, *one at rest*, the original (*ein Ruhender*) evokes the German title for a pose often found in classical art (e.g. Praxiteles' *Resting Faun*).

Page 13 | 'Hohenburg'

Second version

Title, *Hohenburg*, Schloß Hohenburg near Innsbruck, the home of the Austrian musicologist Rudolf von Ficker, where Trakl stayed as a guest in 1913 and 1914 during bouts of depression.

Page 14 | 'Sebastian Dreaming'

Dedication, *Adolf Loos* (1870–1933), Austrian architect, whose Viennese circle included many artists and writers, among them Oskar Kokoschka and Georg Trakl.

Line 1:15, *Saint Peter's*, the cemetery and catacombs at the base of the Festungsberg, a hill overlooking the city of Salzburg.

Line 2:7, *mountain of Calvary* (Kalvarienberg), an allusion to both the New Testament's Golgotha and the Kalvarienberg, one of Salzburg's prominent hills and a pilgrimage site which features the Stations of the Cross and life-size statues of the crucifixion.

Page 18 | 'On the Moor'

Third version

Page 20 | 'Evening in Lans'

Second version

Title, *Lans*, small village near Innsbruck, Austria.

Page 21 | 'On the Mönchsberg'

Second version

Title, *the Mönchsberg*, a hill overlooking Salzburg named for the Benedictine Abbey there and facing the Kalvarienberg.

Page 22 | 'Kaspar Hauser Song'

Title, *Kaspar Hauser Song*, Trakl's title suggests Paul Verlaine's 1873 poem 'Gaspard Hauser chante' (Gaspard Hauser Sings), which is also inspired by the mysterious German youth Kaspar Hauser (1812(?)–33), who appeared in Nuremberg in 1828 claiming to have grown up in isolation in a dark cell.

Dedication: *Bessie Loos*, Elizabeth Bruce (1886–1921) was a Viennese cabaret dancer (*Tabarin*) and companion of the Austrian architect Adolf Loos

Line 10, *I want to be a horse soldier*, one of Hauser's first utterances, which ended with 'as my father was'.

Line 13, *murderer*, in December 1833, Hauser died of a stab wound that he attributed to a murder attempt but was likely self-inflicted in order to revive his lapsed celebrity.

Line 15, *the just*, an allusion to the defence of Hauser's pathological lying made ironical in that he does not sleep the 'sleep of the just' in the next lines, a maxim that is alluded to as well in the original German.

Line 22, *unborn's head*, possibly a reference to the legend of Hauser's origins, that he was the princely heir of the House of Baden who died at birth.

Page 25 | 'Transfiguration of Evil'

Second version

Page 32 | 'A Winter Evening'

First version

Page 33 | 'The Damned'

Line 11, *scribbler*, pejorative rendering of the original (*Schreiber*, i.e. writer) and a self-deprecatory cameo of the poet himself.

Line 36, *Sonia*, an allusion to the good prostitute in *Crime and Punishment*. Dostoyevsky's heroine is not a child, however.

Page 37 | 'Along'

Line 12, *barrel organ* (*Orgelgeleier*), the German word *Geleier* in the nineteenth- and early-twentieth-century sense was a disparaging term associated with the droning or grinding of a street organ (indeed, some dictionaries define *Geleier* as such) and a 'faithful' or literal translation here would not convey this sense.

Page 39 | 'Afra'

Second version

Title, *Afra*, St Afra (d. 304) was a devotee of Aphrodite and a temple prostitute in Roman Augsburg. During the persecutions of Diocletian, she converted to Christianity and was burnt at the stake for refusing to worship pagan idols.

Page 44 | 'Anif'

Title, *Anif*, a suburb of Salzburg and site of the Anif Water Palace.

Line 4, *hill's just measure*, the Hellbrunner Berg.

Line 5, *green river*, the Salzach River.

Page 47 | 'Going Down'

Fifth version

Title, *Going Down*, the ductility of the original (*Untergang*) is such that it can be read literally as rendered, and figuratively—doom, decline (social and political)—and various forms of sinking, from a wreck (as in the *Titanic*) to a sunset, a cadence in music and so on.

Dedication, *Karl Borromaeus Heinrich* (1884–1938), German diplomat, poet, novelist, essayist and an editor of and contributor to *Die Brenner*. Heinrich and Trakl were close friends and drinking companions to the extent that the latter dedicated two poems to Heinrich.

Line 8, *arching thorns* (*Dornenbogen*), an earlier usage by nineteenth-century German poet Karl Mayer suggests the 'bramble arches' of Victorian English literature, i.e. arching blackberry vines, brier branches, bramble canes and the like. Trakl's usage, however, is more abstract and symbolic. One could see here, too, the tick marks on a clock.

Line 12, *blind* (*blinde*), the original means, as well as unseeing, unseen, false and blind drunk.

Page 48 | 'To One Short-Lived'

Line 6, *the Mönchsberg*, a hill overlooking Salzburg; its environs also include a cemetery, catacombs and parkland, with wooded paths, steps and bridges leading to a plateau that consists of woods and meadows. This translation is dedicated to Daniel Simko.

Page 50 | 'Ghostly Twilight'

Second version

Page 51 | 'Evening Land Song'

Title, *Evening Land*, other renderings of this poem translate the title as 'Song of the West' and the like (or, infelicitously, 'Occident Song'). As rendered here, almost literally, such an allusive title retains its cultural meanings, that the *Abendland* (*evening land*, the West, the Occident), as opposed to the *Morgenland* (*morning land*, the East, the Orient) is where the sun sets, where the dead go, where Christendom rules and so on. That 'Evening Land' meant the West in English is well established if rare now (e.g. Shelley, who alluded to America as the 'Evening-Land' in his verse drama *Hellas*).

Page 55 | 'The Wanderer'

Second version

Page 56 | 'Karl Kraus'

Title, *Karl Kraus* (1874–1936), Austrian writer and cultural journalist.

Page 58 | 'Passion'

Third version

Page 62 | 'Winter Night'

Third paragraph, *Avanti!*, Italian loan word and military parlance, to charge or advance on a position.

Page 68 | 'Limbo'

Line 24, *Chattels*, the original (*Gerät*) relies on context for its meaning, which here would be any kind of useful property, either for the household, workplace and the like, even luggage for travel.

Page 75 | 'Evening Land'

Fourth version

Dedication, *Else Lasker-Schüler* (1869–1945), German poet and one of the few prominent women in the Expressionist movement. Trakl met Lasker-Schüller in Berlin in March 1914 during a visit to his sister, Margarete Jeanne Trakl (1891–1917), called 'Gretl'.

Page 78 | 'Spring of the Soul'

Line 22, *The soul is a strange thing on the earth*, the philosopher Martin Heidegger, in his 1953 essay on Trakl, 'Language in the Poem', responds to this key phrase, which he does not see as alienation per se, but as the 'soul' seeking the earth, moving *towards it and not away*.

Page 81 | 'Song of the Solitary'

Title, *Solitary* (*Abgeschiedene*), i.e. from all living things and one's own ego, that virtue expressed by Meister Eckhart (and later Heidegger) in being a loner, wanderer, outsider, pilgrim, hermit, etc., to the liminal sense of being the departed or one who haunts.

Line 19, *Measure and law*, possibly a direct allusion to Nietzsche's statement in *Introduction to Metaphysics*, that the 'artistic states are those which place themselves under the supreme command of measure and law, taking themselves beyond themselves in their will to advance'.

Page 85 | 'Dream and Benightment'

Title: *Benightment* (*Umnachtung*), the emphasis is placed on darkness, both in the physical and mental sense, of not knowing and madness.

First paragraph: *family* (*Geschlecht*), a ductile word related to procreation (lineage, family, breed, species, race, kind), gender and sexual organs, which can be rendered with an ear to context; chords (*Akkorde*), i.e. the cadence and length of the stride.

Third paragraph, *Jewish girl* (*Judenmädchen*), a Janus word in that *Judenmädchen* can also mean a Jew's girl, i.e. a gentile servant or even prostitute (*Judendirne*) and thus assume a certain opprobrium (*Schickse*).